The Little Caterpillar Afraid of Change

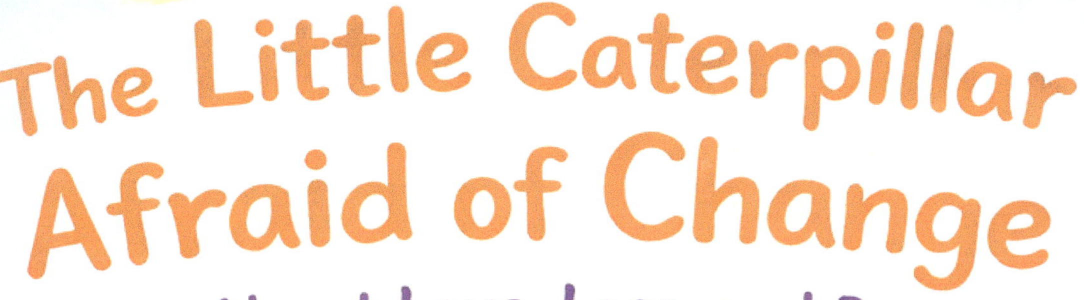

A Story About Love, Loss, and Becoming

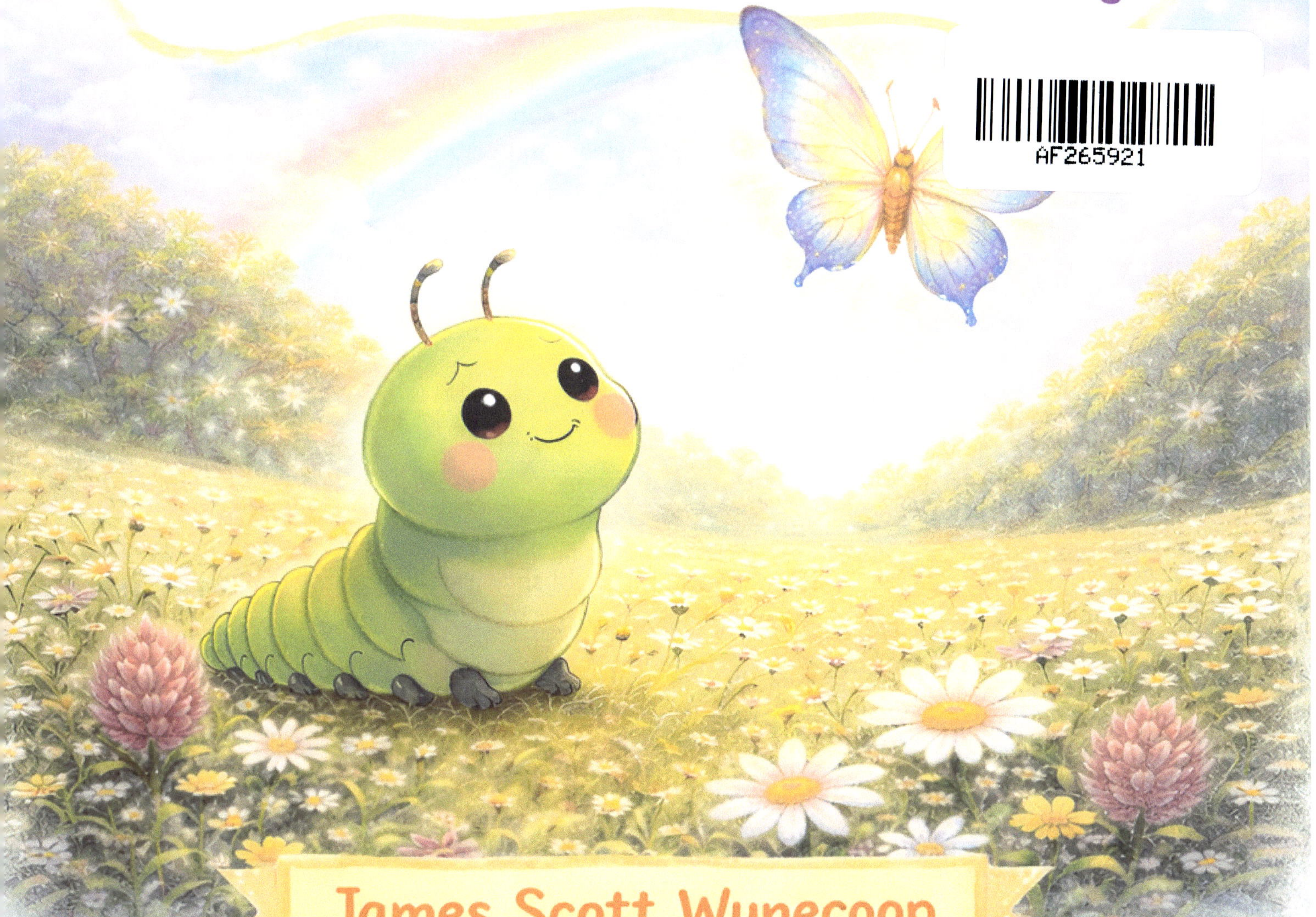

James Scott Wynecoop

Studio of Books LLC
5900 Balcones Drive Suite 100
Austin, Texas 78731
www.studioofbooks.org
Hotline: (254) 800-1183

Ordering Information:
Special discounts are available on quantity purchases by corporations, associations, and others. For details, contact the publisher at the address above.

Printed in the United States of America.

ISBN-13: Softcover: 978-1-970283-87-7
eBook: 978-1-970283-87-7

A Note for Parents and Caregivers

When someone a child loves is no longer here, the questions can be simple... but the feelings are not.

Children do not need complicated explanations. They need something they can understand, something they can feel.

This story offers a gentle way to understand change through nature and love.

Love does not disappear. It changes... and stays with us.

There once was a little caterpillar named Willow.

She spent her days with her best friend, River.

They did everything together.

But one day, River began to feel different.

He became slower and quiet.

He wrapped himself inside a shell.

Willow waited.

The shell stayed still.

Days passed.

Willow felt alone.

Then one day, something changed.

A butterfly emerged.

It rose into the sky.

Willow felt warmth in her heart.

She knew River had gone somewhere beautiful.

Author's Note

Children understand more than we realize, but in their own way.

This story was written to help children understand change without fear.

Through simple imagery, it reminds us that love does not disappear—it changes and remains with us.

www.ingramcontent.com/pod-product-compliance
Lightning Source LLC
Chambersburg PA
CBHW042130030726
47599CB00002B/415

* 9 7 8 1 9 7 0 2 8 3 8 7 7 *